Christians Laugh Too
The Christian life through cartoons and Humor

Joseph Brown

ISBN: 0-9861025-1-2
ISBN-13: 978-0-9861025-1-6

DEDICATION

This book is dedicated to Robin, my wife and best friend.

CONTENTS

INTRODUCTION

This collection of cartoons is intended to create a smile, snicker or laugh, but they serve another purpose, that is to communicate biblical truths and the Christian values we should be trying to uphold. We all need reminders that Jesus wants us to represent him in our words and actions. These cartoons do that and can also be used to share God's goodness with others. When Christians laugh, too, it is a great witness to the world that being a child of God is a joyful experience. I hope you enjoy these and share them as much as possible; there should be room on the fridge for at least one.

Peace and blessings,

Joe

CHURCHY CARTOONS

"Hey Frank, any plans after church?"

"I mistakenly stood in the doorway when kid's church let out."

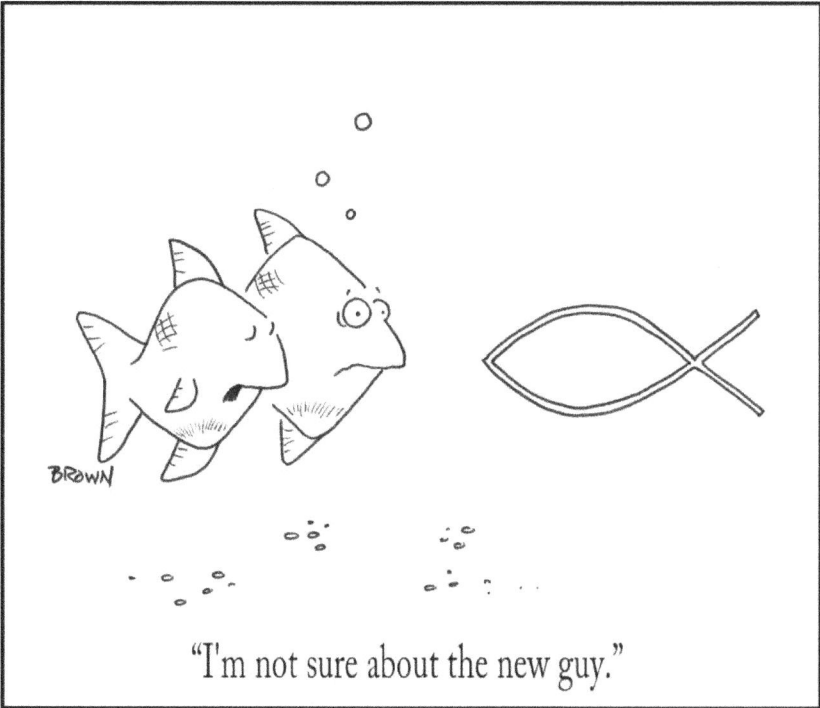

"I'm not sure about the new guy."

"There is no WI-FI. It's a flannel board."

"Jesus forgave you because he had to."

"As a member of the Sunday praise team you are not allowed to "change it up", whenever you feel led."

"It's fine as long as he stays behind me."

"Is this communion wafer gluten-free?"

"These choir robes are so hot, I'm glad I went commando."

"I hate how hypocrites always gossip about others, like Bob for example. Do you know Bob..."

"It's bad enough you left your phone on during the church service, but did "Highway to Hell" have to be your ringtone?"

Make this quick. I can only hold my breath for 17 seconds.

Baptisms should always have ground rules.

"What's the current return on investment?"

"Think about it, if it were not for evil we would be out of a job."

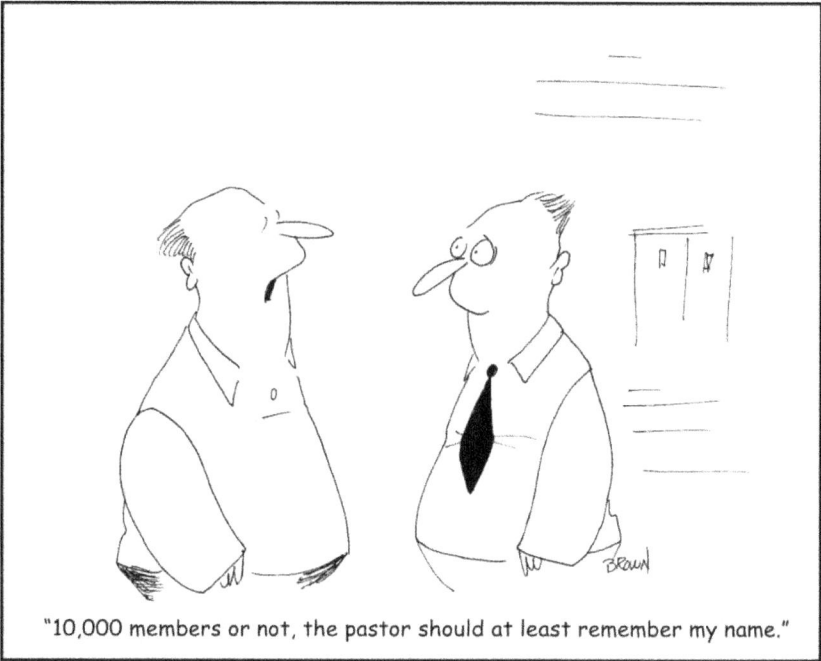

"10,000 members or not, the pastor should at least remember my name."

"It's my life line in case the Rapture happens, so I'm not left behind."

"Oh, that's a missionary school."

Sir, booing the pastor is not allowed.

"Your sermon started out strong, then it got a little slow and I nodded off."

Son of God or not, no one comes to church dressed like that.

"We are considering a nursery expansion."

"Hold on there; didn't we just do this last week?"

"No, anointing oil does not come in different grades depending on the application."

"Maybe we should change the name of the parish to something cool, like the Protestants do and add a coffee bar."

"It's not that we consider ourselves holier than others just because we choose to sit in the front row."

"You must be the pastor's kid I've heard so much about."

"Following Jesus has nothing to do with Twitter."

Bob, you've been warned before. You can't come to prayer just to gather gossip material.

When church potlucking, Harold prefers quantity over quality.

When raising hands in worship, use of deodorant is critical, especially when seated next to visitors.

"It helps with the reception."

"I choose not to read Revelations, too many spoilers."

Ministry 101: Never perform a baptism in a river with a strong current.

Please follow safe worship practices.

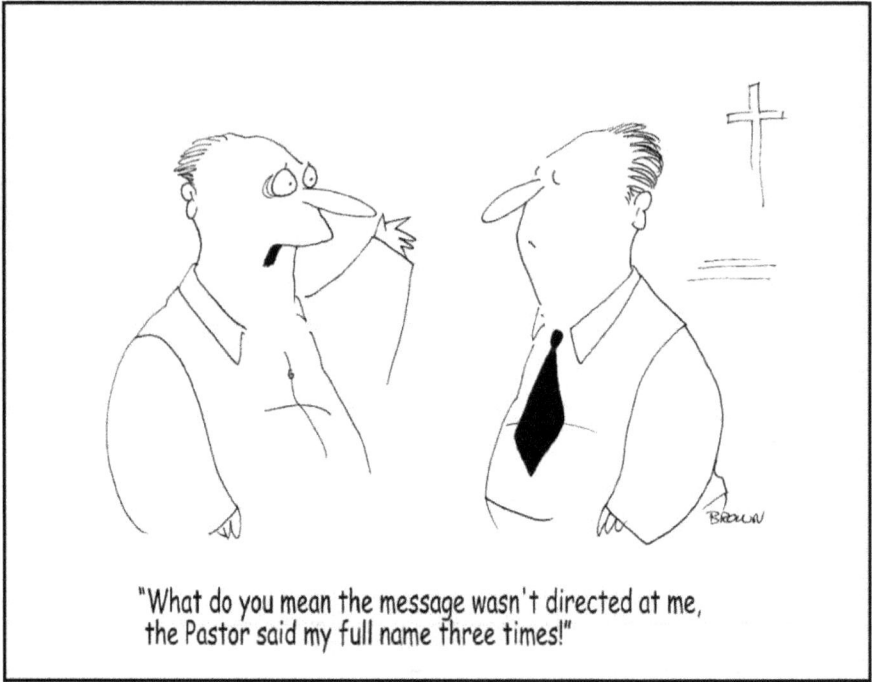

"What do you mean the message wasn't directed at me, the Pastor said my full name three times!"

"One more, "get thee behind me Satan" and you'll experience "death do us part"!"

"We were forced to leave our last church when some visitors took our seats."

"Is this guy serious?"

"If God tells you what to say in your sermon, why do you make so many corrections?"

"I know filled with the spirit, and you most certainly are not."

"Would you like seating in snoring or non-snoring?"

"I love social media, it makes gossip so efficient."

"Henry, stop staring at the visitors. They didn't know that's where we usually sit."

"If God wanted me to go to church, he wouldn't have put football on Sundays."

"Sword drills just aren't the same since Bible apps."

"If you know whats good for you, you'll go forward at the altar call..."

"Do you honestly believe we evolved from a single snow flake?"

OLDER TESTAMENT CARTOONS

Lazarus does some explaining.

"Really Adam, you need that big of a fig leaf..."

Meeting up with Rex, Adam immediately counted his ribs.

"That better not be a second rib scar, Adam ."

One day at the river, Cain and Able notice adam is belly buttonless.

If Adam and Eve were Baptist.

"Eve, if I tell you something can you keep it a secret?"

"Adam, I have a bone to pick with you!"

"But Eve, I really do think you're the most beautiful woman in the world."

"Are you going to accept my friend request or not, Adam?"

"Look at my new laptop, Adam..."

"Don't worry, it's organic..."

One bar of service. At least in Egypt we had a better signal.

The Israelites begin to grumble.

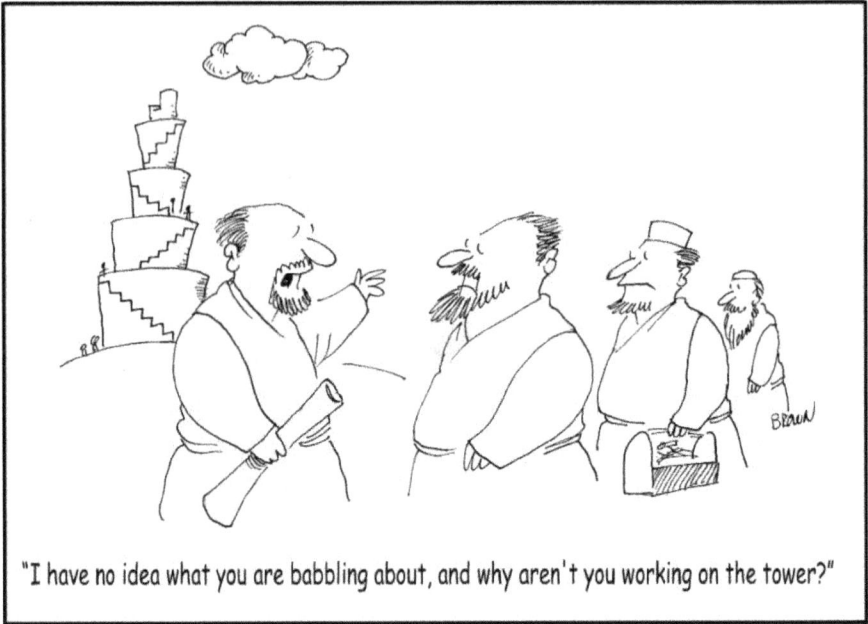

"I have no idea what you are babbling about, and why aren't you working on the tower?"

So, David. Do you have a permit for that weapon?

"Daniel, I seem to have dropped my keys,
could you look around and toss them up."

"Now be careful Goliath or you will shoot your eye out."

Goliath's fateful decision.

"No, no. I said Bathsheba!"

Absalon's bad hair day.

Jacob's first attempt at deceiving Isaac.

"With you around Sampson will always have a jawbone handy if needed."

"Sorry, but you didn't purchase the extended warranty that covered Hebrews."

Visiting the aquarium was never the same for Jonah after the Nineveh incident.

Ironic, but in college Jonah was the goldfish swallowing champion.

Jonah met a strange wooden boy in the belly of the whale.

"Let's get our story straight. Was it a whale or a big fish?"

"But it's not the King James Version."

"Honestly, there were 15 but I dropped a tablet."

Moses' first encounter with the burning bush didn't go well.

"For the last time Pharaoh, it's a plague, not global warming."

Moses attempted to initiate the frog plague on his own.

After 39 years, 11 months and 29 days, Moses finally received the GPS he ordered.

"I'm not sure Moses; it just doesn't sound right."

"This cruise would have been a lot more fun if Noah had invited female unicorns too."

"well, there goes the new ark smell."

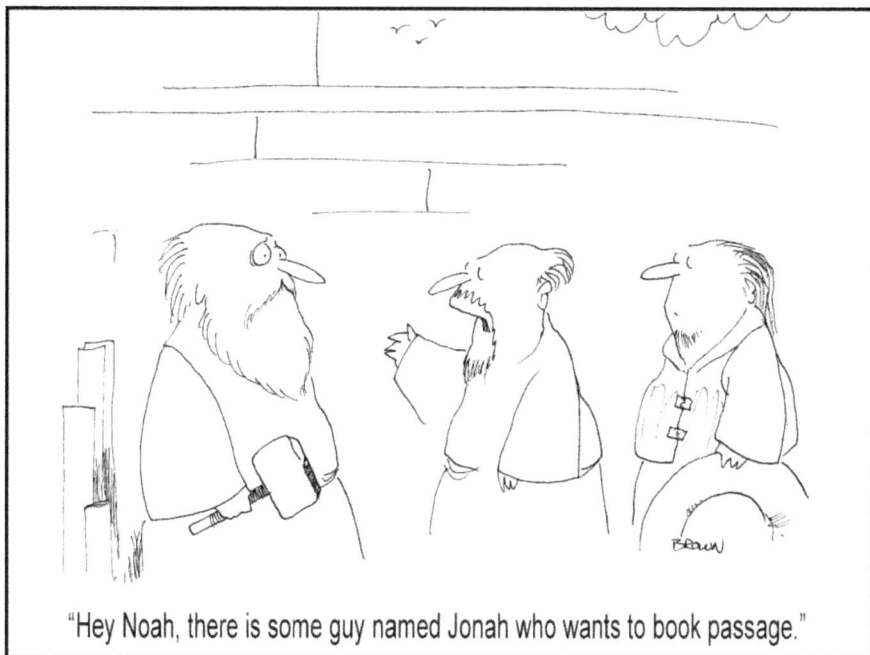

"Hey Noah, there is some guy named Jonah who wants to book passage."

"Great, a lottery ticket. I was hoping for something more like an olive branch."

Tempers flair on the ark.

Noah tires of his dog.

"Better work the legs next time at the gym, Sampson."

The humidity plays heck with Sampson's hair.

"I just glanced back at Sodom & Gomorrah for a second..."

"I'm sorry but this is a staff meeting and that is obviously a rod..."

Have you been in the valley of dry bones again?

Ezekiel and his dog.

NEWER TESTAMENT CARTOONS

Matthew, Mark, Luke, Peter. John you are out of order again.

"Save the loaves for the other 4,999. I am gluten intolerant."

"Now all we need is 5,000 packets of tartar sauce!"

"Don't take this wrong, we 5,000 are appreciative of the food, we just thought next time a little variety might be nice."

No, I didn't know there was a bad Samaritan.

"Yes, we are disciples and, no, our names are not John, Jacob, Jingleheimer Schmidt."

Jesus plays peek-a-boo with doubting Thomas.

If you just walk out on the water a little ways, you could catch us some great pokemon.

The disciples get caught up in the latest craze.

The first Baptist potluck was less than successful since John only brought locusts.

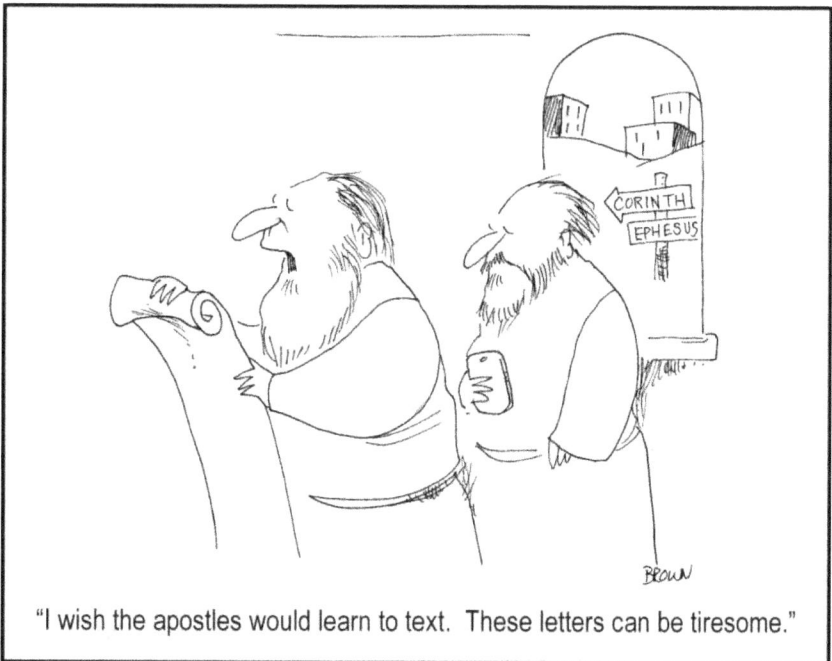

"I wish the apostles would learn to text. These letters can be tiresome."

Original versus contemporary short term missionary

John is asked what church he attends.

"WAIT!"

"Do I have one too?"

"I tried the old, if you're without sin throw the first stone.
Well, figures Jesus was in the crowd."

"Turning the water into wine was amazing,
now how about some fruit punch for the kids."

Jesus takes his first contemporary communion.

Jesus' lesser known miracle at the wedding

Jesus, the original paddleboarder.

Jesus was banned from all future fishing tournaments.

So Jesus, do you prefer Methodist or Lutheran?

"Sorry Judas, we only came up with 29 pieces of silver."

"Judas, where did you get these 30 pieces of candy?"

Jesus always enjoyed a day on the water fishing.

Motors shot, Looks like you'll be rowing the boat ashore Michael.

"I forget is it a star or a planet that blinks..."

Frank reads "like sheep to slaughter..."
for the first time.

The real reason Zacchaeus was up the tree.

UP OR DOWN CARTOONS

"I hate churches with ceiling fans."

"Lets make this quick; I've had a bad day."

"I remember behavior like that being followed by fire and brimstone."

"You again, what is this the seventh time."

"You'll get used to it."

"Sometimes I miss a good smiting."

"Martha, he's back."

"I saw your eye twitch, I knew you were lying."

You always said all doors lead to the same place, so just pick one.

"No, there are no emergency exits!"

IN CASE
OF
FIRE
PULL

"I'm afraid you have a visitor."

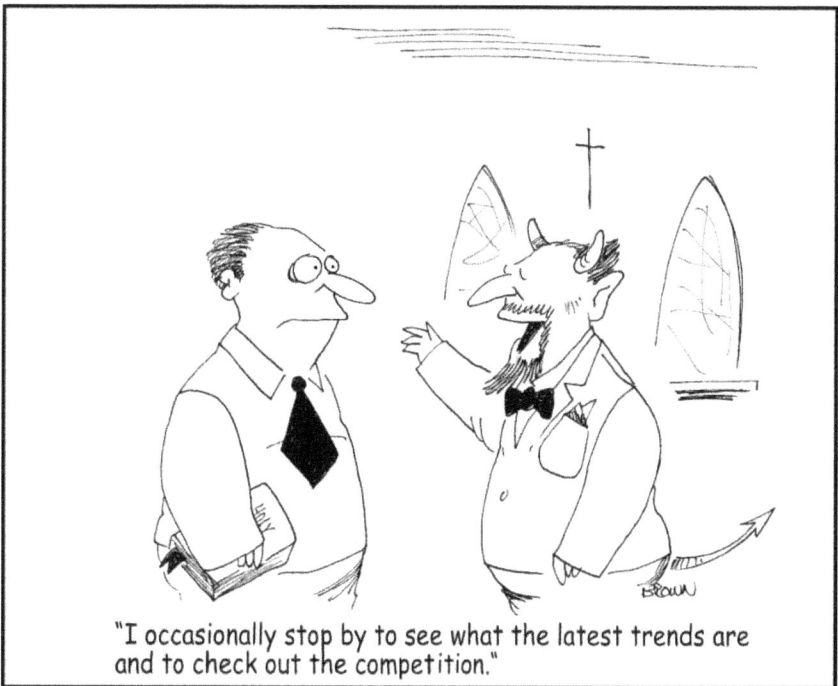

"I occasionally stop by to see what the latest trends are and to check out the competition."

"MAC or PC?"

Wait, there you are. I was just spelling it wrong.

"Of course we allow texting, just not thumbs..."

"Two subjects are off limits; religion and politics."

"I can never remember if it's smite or smote."

"I may have to let you in, but that doesn't mean I'm happy about it."

"Going up or down?"

"They never would have got away with that in the Old Testament."

"The thing is, it really sucks down here."

"I caught one. I actually caught one."

"It's the newest upgrade."

"Personally, I think the cumulus taste more cotton candy then marshmallow..."

"And then there was the time you told your mom to shut up."

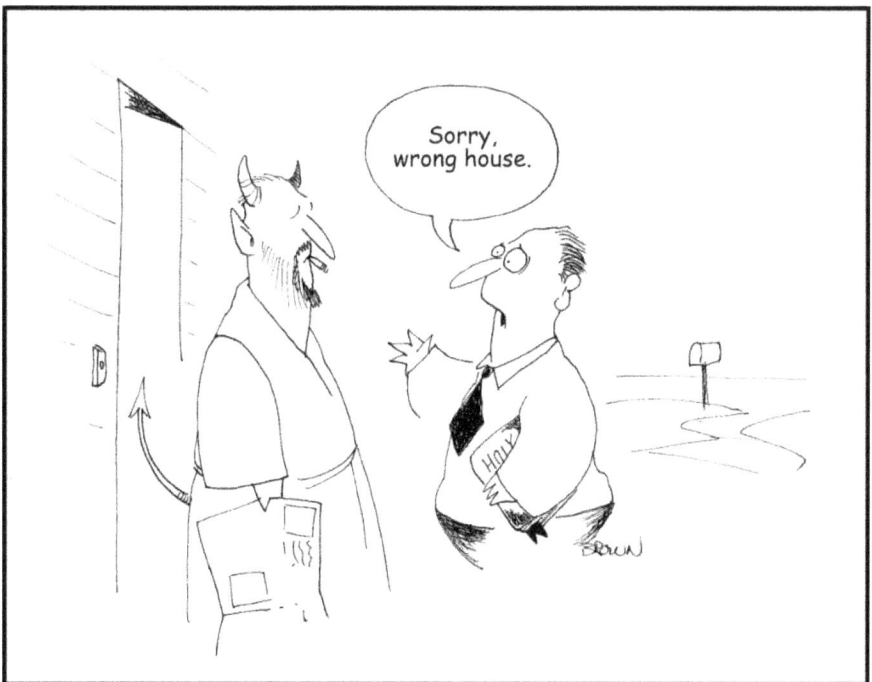

Sorry, wrong house.

"GOOEY GUMMY BEARS"
BOOK EXCERPT: *CRAZY PASTOR'S WIFE*
AUTHOR: JOYCE THRASHER
ILLUSTRATOR: JOE BROWN

My son Zach and I love gummy bears, so often I'll buy a three pound bag of them for us. He likes the green and red ones and I like the orange and yellow ones, so it all works out well.

Last year when I opened up a three pound bag, I ripped the top so much that the bag wouldn't close again. That evening when we went to church, the gummy bears were left on the kitchen counter, totally exposed in the ripped open bag. When we got home from church, I put them in a Ziploc bag.

A little later Zach and his girlfriend were eating gummy bears, and had consumed almost half of the three pound bag. They commented, "Something's wrong. These gummy bears don't taste right." My brother Joe was visiting from Michigan at that time and he also was eating gummy bears by the handful, just shoving them into his mouth. When he came up for air, he, too, said, "Yeah, these gummy bears don't taste right." Even so, Joe continued to feast!

I don't know why, but suddenly I wondered if my cat had "done his business" on the gummy bears. Sure enough, when I checked (and smelled) the remaining gummy bears in the bag, it was evident that that's what had happened. Fluffy had peed on them! At that exact moment, when Zach and his girlfriend had a mouth full of gummy bears, I laughed almost uncontrollably and told them why they didn't taste right. They spit them out immediately. And Joe? He spewed gummy bears out of his mouth and they hit the wall across the kitchen. Really? It was only a little cat dribble!

Sometimes things, just like those gummy bears, look good, but they aren't. That's how sin is. It can look really good on the outside, but when we give in to it, we find out it doesn't "taste" so good. So the next time you think about doing something that looks good, but you know it isn't right, think about the gummy bears and remember this: not everything tastes as good as it looks!

Do you like honey? Don't eat too much, or it will make you sick! (Proverbs 25:16 NLT)

JOYCE THRASHER

Joyce (Joe's sister) is a retired pastor's wife now travelling the country in an RV visiting churches and doing speaking engagements. She is working on her second book on life as a pastor's wife and I wouldn't be surprised if there is a third relating to the RV life. She can be reached at www, crazypastorswife.com

ABOUT THE AUTHOR

Joe Brown is a freelance cartoonist featured in numerous periodicals and books. He has been cartooning for decades and is a pastel artist too. He recently collaborated with his sister, Joyce Thrasher illustrating her book *Crazy Pastor's Wife*. Look for more of Joe's work at www.christianslaughtoo.com

www.ingramcontent.com/pod-product-compliance
Lightning Source LLC
Chambersburg PA
CBHW070543030426
42337CB00016B/2325